WORD
Made
FLESH

"The entirety of the scriptures—from Genesis to Revelation—recounts the story of God's profound love for his creation. Christopher West's *Word Made Flesh* provides an ongoing reflection on this love through the lens of St. John Paul II's catechesis on the nuptial meaning of creation. Since these meditations follow the Sunday Lectionary, every Catholic can benefit from this companion as they pray their way through the liturgical year."

Most Rev. Kevin C. Rhoades
Bishop of Fort Wayne–South Bend

"Christopher West does it again! Through the lens of Theology of the Body, he helps break open the Sunday readings to reveal the deep mysteries of our desires. Let him personally walk alongside you each week and you will find your heart burning within you."

Rose Sweet
Catholic author, speaker, and retreat leader

"Christopher West's new book has been a secret dream of many familiar with Theology of the Body, including myself. So many liturgical Bible readings lend themselves to an explication through the lens of St. John

Paul II's masterwork, and now West has connected the dots. As Catholics, we have three sources of Revelation: Creation (the Father), Scripture (the Son), the Church (the Holy Spirit). In *Word Made Flesh*, West, with his gift of clarity, helps us to discern all three sources working together and assists both clergy and laity in breaking open the Word of God in all its physical and spiritual richness and beauty."

Sr. Helena Burns, F.S.P.
Theology of the Body presenter

WORD
Made
FLESH

A Companion to the Sunday Readings
(Cycle C)

Christopher West

AVE MARIA PRESS AVE Notre Dame, Indiana

To my mother, Marian (Bonnie) West,
who has dedicated her life valiantly to
incarnating the Word.

ACKNOWLEDGMENTS

My sincere thanks go to Bill Howard who first proposed the idea of turning my weekly reflections on the Sunday readings into a book. He worked diligently to get this off the ground and bring it to fruition.

Phillip Rolfes was a godsend in all the work he did organizing the manuscript, pulling scripture quotes, and providing scripture references. Thank you!

My thanks also to Ian Rutherford who recommended Ave Maria Press as the right fit for this kind of book.

Finally, my thanks to everyone at Ave Maria Press who embraced this project and brought it to publication.

INTRODUCTION

Christianity is the religion of the "Word" of God, a word which is "not a written and mute word, but the Word is incarnate and living" (St. Bernard). If the Scriptures are not to remain a dead letter, Christ, the eternal Word of the living God, must, through the Holy Spirit, "open [our] minds to understand the Scriptures" (Lk 24:45).

—*Catechism of the Catholic Church*, 108

The sacred words of scripture are, of course, critically important to our faith. "Still, the Christian faith is not a 'religion of the book,'" as the *Catechism* insists (108). It is the religion of the Divine Word that "became flesh and made his dwelling among us" (Jn 1:14). Scripture, in fact, will remain a dead letter unless every word of it is read in view of the Word made flesh.

That is the purpose of the volume you now hold in your hands. Inspired by the scriptural vision St. John Paul II unfolded for us in his 129 Wednesday audiences from 1979 to 1984 that came to be known as the "Theology of the Body" (TOB), the brief, prayerful reflections on the Sunday readings in this book are intended to "open [our] minds to understand the Scriptures" by reading them in light of "the Word [which] is incarnate and living."

ULTIMATE MEANING IS MADE FLESH

Have you ever paused to ponder what the Bible actually means by referring to the eternal Son of God as the Word? "Word" does not quite convey all the richness of the Greek *logos*. "Logos" refers to the rational principle governing the universe—the ultimate meaning, reason, logic, and beauty behind *everything*. And the astounding claim upon which all of Christianity rests is that the human body is God's chosen vehicle for communicating his Word, for communicating ultimate meaning, and for communicating who he is, who we are, and his final plan for the universe.

Just as in Jesus' day, when people hear how important the body is to Christian faith, they often respond as did some of the first disciples: "This saying is hard; who can accept it?" (Jn 6:60). This response is understandable. How could something as earthly as the human body convey something as heavenly as the mystery of God? And yet, if we believe in the meaning of Christmas, we should also believe this claim. For those with eyes to see, our bodies are not only biological; they're theological—they reveal the logic of God; they reveal the ultimate meaning behind everything.

This is why St. John Paul II's Theology of the Body, despite how it is typically framed, is not merely a papal teaching on marital love and human sexuality. It is that, to be sure, but it is also so much more. As John Paul II himself said, what we learn in his TOB "concerns the entire Bible" (TOB 69:8) and plunges us into "the perspective of the whole Gospel, of the whole teaching of the whole mission of Christ" (TOB 49:3). Through the lens of spousal love, St. John Paul II's Theology of the Body leads to "the rediscovery of the meaning of the whole of existence . . . the meaning of life" (TOB 46:6).

Having spoken since the 1990s to Catholic audiences around the world, it is clear to me that we are often unaware of what is really happening in the liturgy. We "look but do not see and hear but do no listen or understand," as Jesus is quoted saying in Matthew 13:13. Reflecting on the Sunday Mass readings with the help of St. John Paul II's Theology of the Body is like putting on a pair of glasses that brings the entire biblical story (and the liturgy itself) into focus. Familiar passages and parables suddenly "pop open," enabling us to enter their inner mystery and meaning as never before. We come to see that the whole of the Christian life is an invitation—as Jesus proposed in Matthew 22:1–14 and Luke 14:15–24—to a wedding feast!

GOD WANTS TO MARRY US

Scripture uses many images to help us understand God's love for us. Each image has its own valuable place. But as John Paul II shared, the gift of Christ's body on the Cross gives "definitive prominence to the spousal meaning of God's love" (*Mulieris Dignitatem* 26). In fact, from the beginning to end, the Bible tells a nuptial or marital story. It begins in Genesis with the marriage of the first man and woman, and it ends in Revelation with the marriage of Christ and the Church. Right in the middle of the Bible, we find the erotic poetry of the Song of Songs. These bookends and this center-piece provide the key for reading and understanding the whole biblical story. Indeed, we can summarize all of sacred scripture with five simple yet astounding words: *God wants to marry us*. Consider:

> For as a young man marries a virgin,
>   your Builder shall marry you;
> And as the bridegroom rejoices in his bride
>   so shall your God rejoice in you.
> (Is 62:5)

> I will betroth you to me forever:
> I will betroth you to me with justice and
>   with judgment
>   with loyalty and with compassion;
> I will betroth you to me with fidelity.
> (Hos 2:19)

God is inviting each of us, in a unique and unrepeatable way, to an unimagined intimacy with him, akin to the intimacy of spouses in one flesh. In fact, as Pope Francis observed, "the very word [used in scripture to describe marital union] . . . 'to cleave' . . . is used to describe our union with God: 'My soul clings to you' (Ps 63:8)." Because of the supreme bliss of union with God, "a love lacking either pleasure or passion is insufficient to symbolize the union of the human heart with God: 'All the mystics have affirmed that supernatural love and heavenly love find the symbols which they seek in marital love'" (*Amoris Laetitia* 13, 142).

While we may need to work through some discomfort or even fear to reclaim the true sacredness, the true holiness of the imagery, the "scandalous" truth is that scripture describes "God's passion for his people using boldly erotic images" as Pope Benedict XVI explained in *Deus Caritas Est* (9). Elsewhere he declared, "*Eros* is part of God's very Heart: the Almighty awaits the 'yes' of his creatures as a young bridegroom that of his bride" (Lenten Message 2007).

We are probably more familiar (and more comfortable) describing God's love as "agape"—the Greek word for sacrificial, self-giving love. Yet God's love "may certainly be called eros," asserted Pope Benedict XVI. In Christ, eros is "supremely ennobled . . . so purified as to become one with agape." Thus, the Bible has no qualms employing the erotic poetry of the Song of Songs as a description of "God's relation to man and man's relation to God." In this way, as Pope Benedict XVI concluded, the Song of Songs became not only an expression of the intimacies of marital love but also "an expression of the essence of biblical faith: that man can indeed enter into union with God—his primordial aspiration" (*Deus Caritas Est* 10).

THE ESSENCE OF BIBLICAL FAITH

Let's try to let this essential message sink in: *the Song of Songs, this unabashed celebration of erotic love, express-es the essence of biblical faith.* How so? The essence of biblical faith is that God came among us in the flesh not only to forgive our sins (as astounding as that gift is); he became "one flesh" with us so we could share in his eternal exchange of love. In the first of his many sermons on the Song of Songs, St. Bernard of Clairvaux aptly described marriage as "the sacrament of endless union with God." The book of Revelation calls this endless union the "marriage of the Lamb" (Rv 19:7).

But there is more. Remember that pithy rhyme we learned as children: "First comes love, then comes marriage, then comes the baby in the baby carriage"? We probably didn't realize as children that we were actually reciting some profound theology. Yes, our bodies tell a divine story; our bodies tell the story that God loves us, wants to marry us, and wants us to "conceive" eternal life within us. This is not merely a metaphor.

Representing all of us, a young Jewish woman named Mary once gave her yes to God's marriage proposal with such totality and fidelity that she literally conceived eternal life in her womb. In a hymn addressed to her, St. Augustine exclaimed, "The Word becomes united with flesh, he makes his covenant with flesh, and your womb is the sacred bed on which this holy union of the Word with flesh is consummated" (Sermon 291). Mary's virginity has always been understood by the Church as the sign of her betrothal to God. She is the "mystic bride of love eternal," as a traditional hymn has it. As such, Mary perfectly fulfills the spousal character of the human vocation in relation to God (see CCC 505).

PENETRATING THE ESSENCE OF THE MYSTERY

In the midst of unfolding the biblical analogy of spousal love, it is very important to understand the bounds within which we are using such language and imagery. "It is obvious," wrote John Paul II, "that the analogy of . . . human spousal love, cannot offer an adequate and complete understanding of . . . the divine mystery." God's "*mystery remains transcendent with respect to this analogy* as with respect to any other analogy." At the same time, however, St. John Paul II maintains that the spousal analogy allows a certain "penetration" into the very essence of the mystery (see TOB 95b:1). And no biblical author reaches more deeply into this essence than St. Paul in his letter to the Ephesians.

Quoting directly from Genesis, St. Paul states:

> For this reason a man shall leave [his]
> father and [his] mother

> and be joined to his wife,
> and the two shall become one flesh.

Then, linking the original marriage with the ultimate marriage, he adds, "This is a great mystery, and I mean in reference to Christ and the Church" (Eph 5:31–32).

We can hardly overstate the importance of this passage for St. John Paul II and the whole theological tradition of the Church. He called it the "summa" ("sum total") of Christian teaching about who God is and who we are (see *Letter to Families* 19). He said that this passage contains the "crowning" of all the themes in sacred scripture and expresses the "central reality" of the whole of divine revelation (see TOB 87:3). The mystery spoken of in this passage "is 'great' indeed," he said. "It is what God . . . wishes above all to transmit to mankind in his Word." Thus, "one can say that [this] passage . . . 'reveals—in a particular way—man to man, himself and makes his supreme vocation clear'" (TOB 93:2; 87:6).

So what is this "supreme vocation" we have as human beings that Ephesians 5 makes clear? Stammering for words to describe the ineffable, the mystics call it "nuptial union" . . . with God. Christ is the New

Adam who left his Father in heaven. He also left the home of his mother on earth. Why? To mount "the marriage bed of the Cross," as St. Augustine portrayed it, unifying himself with the Church and consummating the union forever.

COME TO THE WEDDING FEAST

The more we allow the brilliant rays of St. John Paul II's Theology of the Body to illuminate our vision, the more we come to understand, as the *Catechism* observes, how the "entire Christian life bears the mark of the spousal love of Christ and the Church. Already Baptism, the entry into the People of God, is a nuptial mystery; it is so to speak the nuptial bath which precedes the wedding feast, the Eucharist" (CCC 1617).

I never met my father-in-law; he died when my wife was a young girl. But I admire him tremendously because of the intuition he had as a brand-new husband. At Mass the day after his wedding, having consummated his marriage the night before, he was in tears as he came back to the pew after receiving the Eucharist. When his new bride inquired about his emotional state, he said, "For the first time in my life I understood the meaning of those words, 'This is my body given for you.'"

This was a man for whom the Word of God was not a dead letter. God's Word had become flesh . . . *in his own flesh*. This was a man who had been given eyes to see and ears to hear what God's Word is in its very essence: an invitation to a Wedding Feast. My prayer is that this companion to the Sunday readings will help do the same for you.

My hope is that you will keep this little volume with you when you go to Sunday Mass. Use it to guide your prayer after Communion. Or better yet, get to Mass early enough to read the day's readings in advance and then use this companion to help you enter into the treasures of that day's liturgy. Like the disciples on the road to Emmaus, Christ is walking with us to "open the scriptures" to us so as to reveal himself to us in the breaking of the bread. Lord, give us ears that hear and eyes that see. Amen.

THE ADVENT
AND CHRISTMAS
SEASONS

FIRST SUNDAY
OF ADVENT

The days are coming, says the LORD, *when I will
fulfill the promise I made to the house of Israel and
Judah.* (*Jeremiah 33:14*)

Terror and Hope at the Coming
of the Bridegroom

Advent is a time in which the Church prepares her
heart for the coming of her Bridegroom, Jesus Christ—
commemorating his first coming in Bethlehem and
anticipating his second coming at the end of time when
her every longing will be fulfilled in the "marriage of the
Lamb." An eternal marriage "is what awaits us," explains
Pope Francis: "And it is not just a manner of speaking: they will be real and true nuptials!" But before his
return, as Christ warns in this Sunday's gospel, nations
will be in dismay because of the calamities befalling the
earth. "But when these signs begin to happen", Jesus
tells us, we should stand tall because our "redemption
is at hand." Pope Benedict XVI reminds us that "the
Last Judgment is not primarily an image of terror, but

an image of hope." It's an image of hope because it's the revelation not only of God's justice and judgment but also of his grace and mercy. "If it were merely justice, in the end it could bring only fear to us all," observes Pope Benedict XVI. But it is Christ the Bridegroom who comes to us with his love. Christ has "linked the two together—judgment and grace." Jesus, teach us how to await your judgment and grace with peace and hope.

Scripture: Jeremiah 33:14–16; Psalm 25:4–5, 8–9, 10, 14; 1 Thessalonians 3:12–4:2; Luke 21:25–28, 34–36

SECOND SUNDAY OF ADVENT

All flesh shall see the salvation of God. (Luke 3:6)

What Do We Worth-ship?

This Sunday's gospel ends with the hopeful proclamation that "all flesh shall see the salvation of God." What is the salvation of God? From what do we need salvation? Sin is the textbook answer. But what is sin? We haven't gotten to sin's essence if we think of it merely as a violation of a law. Sin is every attempt we make to satisfy the desires of our hearts with less than the satisfaction for which we are made. We are made for eternal ecstasy in union with God—what the saints called "nuptial union with the Lord." The joys of this temporal world are meant to point us to that eternal joy, but when we love temporal pleasures more than infinite ones, our values are all mixed up. The salvation that "all flesh shall see" is precisely what St. Paul prays for in the second reading: "That your love may increase ever more and more in knowledge and every kind of perception, to discern what is of value." For when we discern what is of true value—namely, Infinite Love—our desires become reoriented and we come to worship that which is of ultimate worth. "Worship" comes from worthship: that to which we assign ultimate worth. When we let go of lesser values and worth-ship ultimate Value (God), *that* is salvation. It's a painful reorientation, for we all have many God substitutes to which we cling. The hard work involved on this journey, however, ends in rejoicing, as we read in this Sunday's psalm. Those who embrace this journey of purification can truly say,

"The Lord has done great things for us; we are filled with joy!"

Scripture: Baruch 5:1–9; Psalm 126:1–2, 2–3, 4–5, 6; Philippians 1:4–6, 8–11; Luke 3:1–6

THIRD SUNDAY OF ADVENT

Shout for joy, O daughter Zion! Sing joyfully, O Israel! Be glad and exult with all your heart, O daughter Jerusalem! (Zephaniah 3:14)

Shout for Joy: You Are Pregnant with God!

In this Sunday's first reading, we have a powerful prophecy of the eternal nuptials to be consummated between God and humanity within Mary: "Shout for joy, O daughter Zion . . . the King of Israel, the LORD, is in your midst" (Zep 3:14, 15). As Pope Benedict XVI expounds, "Literally it says: 'he is in your womb.'" And St. John Paul II tells us that "in the pages of the

Annunciation . . . the New Covenant is presented to us as the Nuptial Covenant of God with man, the divinity with humanity. . . . God's nuptial love, announced by the prophets, is concentrated on . . . the virgin-bride to whom it is granted conceiving and bearing the Son of God." *This* is the joy of all the earth, the source of all hope and gladness! St. Paul exclaims in the second reading, "Rejoice in the Lord always. I shall say it again: rejoice!" Why? "The Lord is near." How near? He is within us. With Mary as the model, we can say that in some way all members of the Church have become Christ-bearers, pregnant with God. "Let this be known throughout all the earth" (Is 12:5)—God wants to marry us and fill us with eternal life! If we say yes to his proposal, God will "renew [us] in his love" (Zep 3:17), and for all eternity we, with Mary, will "cry out with joy and gladness" (Is 12:6).

Scripture: Zephaniah 3:14–18a; Isaiah 12:2–3, 4, 5–6; Philippians 4:4–7; Luke 3:10–18

FOURTH SUNDAY OF ADVENT

When Christ came into the world, he said: "Sacrifice and offering you did not desire, but a body you prepared for me." (Hebrews 10:5)

The Ultimate Glory of Woman's Body

In this Sunday's second reading, we read this reference to Christ's Incarnation: "Sacrifice and offering you did not desire, but a body you prepared for me." And in the gospel we discover precisely where his body was prepared: "Blessed are you among women, and blessed is the fruit of your womb." In the midst of a world that continually desecrates the female body, it is powerfully healing and redemptive to recognize that Christmas celebrates the ultimate glory of a woman's body, and Mary reveals what that ultimate glory is: *God comes to us through the female body*. To recognize this is to be filled with awe and wonder. We share this wonder with the Church that, as St. John Paul II wrote, "honors and praises throughout the centuries 'the womb that bore you and the breasts from which you sucked milk'

(Lk 11:27). "These words," St. John Paul II affirms, "are a eulogy of motherhood, of femininity, of the female body in its typical expression of creative love" (TOB 21:5). As woman goes, so goes the world. And this means the battle for human life is a spiritual contest between the Church's eulogy of the feminine body in its expression of creative love and Satan's desecration of the same. Jesus, show us the true glory of the woman.

Scripture: Micah 5:1–4a; Psalm 80:2–3, 15–16, 18–19; Hebrews 10:5–10; Luke 1:39–45

THE HOLY FAMILY OF JESUS, MARY, AND JOSEPH

See what love the Father has bestowed on us that we may be called the children of God. (1 John 3:1)

Entering Mystically into the Holy Family

Today the Church celebrates the Feast of the Holy Family. The psalm response—"Blessed are they who dwell in your house, O Lord"—is at its mystical depths (all scripture has mystical depths!) an invitation to become an intimate part of the Holy Family. For the house of the Lord is none other than Mary herself— more specifically, it is her womb, where the Lord dwelt for nine months. The psalm proclaims, "How lovely is your dwelling place, O Lord of hosts! My soul yearns and pines for the courts of the Lord." This (again, at its mystical depths) is a yearning to enter the womb of Mary and be reborn there as God's child. (Recall from John 3:4 that when Nicodemus asked if a person could enter his mother's womb a second time, Jesus didn't say no.) Sacramentally we were born of Mary's womb in our baptism. "See what love the Father has bestowed on us that we may be called the children of God. And so we are" (1 Jn 3:1). None of us was raised in a perfect family. But here's the good news: mystically, we can all be "re-mothered" and "re-fathered" in the Holy Family. As followers of Christ, our pilgrimage takes us the whole way through his life, starting with his conception in the womb of Mary and continuing throughout his life in the Holy Family. As the psalm states, "Blessed are they who dwell in your house! . . . Their hearts are set upon the pilgrimage." Lord, guide us on this pilgrimage to your glorious house.

Scripture: Sirach 3:2–6, 12–14 (or 1 Samuel 1:20–22, 24–28); Psalm 128:1–2, 3, 4–5 (or Psalm 84:2–3, 5–6, 9–10); Colossians 3:12–21 (or 1 John 3:1–2, 21–24); Luke 2:41–52

EPIPHANY OF THE LORD

Nations shall walk by your light, and kings by your shining radiance. (Isaiah 60:3)

You Shall Be Radiant at What You See

Today we celebrate the Epiphany of the Lord to the Gentiles. We discover that the magi—Gentiles who journey from a foreign land—are "copartners in the promise in Christ Jesus" (Eph 3:6). As the first reading indicates, the blessings of Jerusalem are not only for the Jews: other nations—sons and daughters—shall walk by the light of the Lord and will come "from afar." In what sense does Jerusalem bear sons and daughters? It is in the spousal mystery of the scriptures that the mystery of Jerusalem (God's holy city and dwelling place) is fulfilled in Mary—who is both the Mother of God and "the Mother of all the living." Enter the first reading from this perspective and the mystery opens to us: "Rise up in splendor, [Mary] . . . the glory of the Lord shines upon you." While darkness covers the rest of the earth, and "thick clouds [cover] the peoples," the Lord shines on Mary and over her "appears his glory." This woman brings God to earth, her body revealing the glory of the Lord to all the kings and nations of the world. If we, like the wise magi, set out on a journey of discovery, we "shall be radiant" at what we see and our "heart shall throb and overflow." Mary, show us the glory of your son.

Scripture: Isaiah 60:1–6; Psalm 72:1–2, 7–8, 10–11, 12–13; Ephesians 3:2–3a, 5–6; Matthew 2:1–12

BAPTISM OF THE LORD

Heaven was opened and the Holy Spirit descended upon him in bodily form like a dove. (Luke 3:21–22)

Christ Makes Baptism a Bath of Rebirth

Today we celebrate the Lord's baptism in the River Jordan. It is a mystery of unfathomable depths—in fact, as the *Catechism* tells us, it is a "nuptial mystery" (CCC 1617). In the second reading, St. Paul speaks of the "generous love of God" that "saved us through the bath of rebirth and renewal by the Holy Spirit." A *generous* love, as the root of the word indicates, is a love that *generates*, that is, a love that gives birth. The Holy Spirit—"the Lord, the giver of life," as we say in the Nicene Creed—is the generous/generating love of God. Natural generation through perishable seed points to the supernatural generation of Baptism in which Christ gives his "imperishable seed" (CCC 1228) to his Church-Bride. She then "brings forth sons [and daughters] . . . to a new and immortal life" (CCC 507). In Baptism we encounter an open exchange between heaven and earth: heaven opens its mysteries to be poured out on earth, and earth opens to receive them. *This* is what occurred in Christ's baptism: "Heaven was opened and the Holy Spirit descended," as we read in the gospel. In turn, earth opened and all her waters were impregnated with the power to give new life.

Blessed are those who are regenerated through water and the Holy Spirit. Lord, help us understand how blessed we are.

Scripture: Isaiah 40:1–5, 9–11 (or Isaiah 42:1–4, 6–7); Psalm 104:1b–2, 3–4, 24–25, 27–28, 29–30 (or Psalm 29:1–2, 3–4, 3, 9–10); Titus 2:11–14; 3:4–7 (or Acts 10:34–38); Luke 3:15–16, 21–22

ORDINARY TIME

SECOND SUNDAY IN ORDINARY TIME

As a young man marries a virgin, your Builder shall marry you; and as a bridegroom rejoices in his bride so shall your God rejoice in you. (Isaiah 62:5)

Christ Invites Us to a Holy Intoxication at the Wedding Feast of Cana

Today's readings are overflowing with the nuptials of heaven and earth. Note the passage from Isaiah 62:5: "As a young man marries a virgin, your Builder shall marry you." God wants to marry us! That's the whole Bible in five words. And we want to marry him—that's what our deepest hunger for love (eros) is all about. But eros often gets off course because we have all "run out of wine." In the Bible, wine is a symbol of divine love (agape). Since the dawn of sin, eros has been cut off from agape. Christ's first miracle, which we read about in today's gospel, is to restore the wine (agape) to eros in superabundance. Superabundance is an understatement: those six jars held twenty to thirty gallons each (see John 2:6). Average it out and that's 150 gallons of "the best wine"—about 750 bottles! And Jesus wants us to drink up! He invites us to a holy intoxication on God's wine so that our entire humanity—body and soul, sexuality and spirituality—becomes enflamed with divine love. Isn't that what the crowd accused the apostles of on Pentecost day when the fire of God's love descended upon them? "They have had too much new wine" (see Acts 2:13–15). Where do we get the idea that Jesus is a party pooper? Lord, show us how to drink deeply of the new wine you offer us.

Scripture: Isaiah 62:1–5; Psalm 96:1–2, 2–3, 7–8, 9–10; 1 Corinthians 12:4–11; John 2:1–11

THIRD SUNDAY IN ORDINARY TIME

God has so constructed the body as to give greater honor to a part that is without it, so that there may be no division in the body, but that the parts may have the same concern for one another. (1 Corinthians 12:24–25)

Which Parts of the Body Deserve
the Greater Honor?

In this weekend's second reading, St. Paul unfolds a powerful analogy between the human body with its many parts and the Church as "the Body of Christ" with its many parts. As Pope Benedict XVI once wrote, understanding the Church as the Body of Christ "makes sense only against the backdrop of the formula from Genesis 2:24: 'The two shall become one flesh.'" St. Paul writes that there are some "parts of the body that we consider less honorable." However, as St. John Paul II makes clear in his Theology of the Body, it is only because of sin that we *think* they are less honorable. In reality, as St. Paul states, God gives "greater honor" to those parts of the body that we think are less honorable "so that there may be no division in the body." No division in the body means unity in the body, which harkens back to Genesis 2:24 and the two becoming "one body." God has bestowed all the greater honor on the parts of the body that call us to this unity—that is, on the parts of the body that distinguish male and female. A mark of the Body of Christ, of true Christianity, is precisely the recognition of the holiness of the human body and the great honor God bestows on those parts of the body that enable male and female to become "one body." Lord, show us the glory you have bestowed on our bodies as male and female.

Scripture: Nehemiah 8:2–4a, 5–6, 8–10; Psalm 19:8, 9, 10, 15; 1 Corinthians 12:12–30; Luke 1:1–4; 4:14–21

FOURTH SUNDAY IN ORDINARY TIME

Love is patient. (1 Corinthians 13:4)

The Patience of Love and the Refusal to Grasp

This Sunday's second reading contains St. Paul's famous hymn to love, which begins, "Love is patient." It is by far the most popular reading chosen for Catholic weddings. What does it mean to say love is patient? Certainly it means that love is willing to bear with others. But there is also something deeper going on. The *Catechism of the Catholic Church* teaches that the "most fundamental passion is love, aroused by the attraction of the good. Love causes a desire for the absent good and the hope of obtaining it; this movement finds completion in the pleasure and joy of the good possessed" (1765). These two sentences from the *Catechism* sum up well the journey of the interior life. Patience (or lack thereof) in attaining the happiness for which we long will determine our entire lot in life. Sin involves a yearning, but in this case it is a refusal to wait on God to grant the yearning or a refusal to believe that he will. Sin, as such, entails an impatient grasping. Oppositely, love is patient, which is another way of saying love trusts in the proper timing of the divine gift. As the psalmist also writes, "You give them their food at the proper time. You open your hand and satisfy the desire of every living thing" (Ps 145:15–16). The Church is the "open Bride" who awaits the coming of her Bridegroom with joyful expectation. Remember, when you are tempted to grasp at satisfaction, "wait for the Lord with courage; be stouthearted, and wait for the Lord" (Ps 27:14).

Scripture: Jeremiah 1:4–5, 17–19; Psalm 71:1–2, 3–4, 5–6, 15, 17; 1 Corinthians 12:31–13:13; Luke 4:21–30

FIFTH SUNDAY
IN ORDINARY TIME

After he had finished speaking, he said to Simon, "Put out into deep water and lower your nets for a catch."
(Luke 5:4)

Put Out into Deep Water

This Sunday's gospel proclaims the famous story of the miraculous catch of fish and of Jesus calling Peter to "put out into deep water" and become a fisher of men. St. John Paul II wrote that the "first condition for 'putting out into deep water' is to cultivate a deep spirit of prayer nourished by a daily listening to the Word of God." He added that the "authenticity of the Christian life is measured by the depth of one's prayer" and that prayer itself is "an art that must be humbly learnt from the lips of the Divine Master." Notice in the gospel reading how Peter both *listens* to and *follows* Christ's teaching—"at your command I will lower the nets." If we trust only in our own efforts, we will "fish all night and catch nothing." Just as a woman cannot conceive children on her own, the Church, as the Bride of Christ, cannot give life to others unless she is in deep communion with her Bridegroom in his passion and suffering. As Pope Benedict XVI observed, "A mother cannot give life to a child without suffering. Each birth requires suffering, is suffering, and becoming a Christian is a birth. . . . We cannot give life to others without giving up our own lives." Lord, take us "into deep water."

Scripture: Isaiah 6:1–2a, 3–8; Psalm 138:1–2, 2–3, 4–5, 7–8; 1 Corinthians 15:1–11; Luke 5:1–11

THE LENT AND
EASTER SEASONS

FIRST SUNDAY OF LENT

He ate nothing during those days, and when they were over he was hungry. (Luke 4:2)

One Does Not Live on Bread Alone

On this first Sunday of Lent, we read of Christ being tempted by Satan in the desert. Imagine your hunger if you hadn't eaten for forty days! "If you are the Son of God, command this stone to become bread." Satan is going for the jugular here: he's assaulting Christ's relationship with the Father; he's assaulting his very identity in relation to God. "Who are you . . . and who is the Father . . . and what is your relationship?" This is *always* Satan's tactic. And hunger brings us right to the heart of the matter. Will the Father provide for our needs? The temptation is to believe he won't. We are born hungry. But the physical hunger of the newborn babe for mother's milk, like Christ's physical hunger after forty days of fasting, is only a sign of our much deeper, much more profound hunger: our hunger for love, for relationship, and for union. That hunger is called *eros*. And true, lasting satisfaction of that hunger does not come from physical food. It comes *only* from relationship with God. By tempting Christ to take satisfaction of his hunger into his own hands, Satan was not only tempting Christ to invert his physical and spiritual needs but also demanding that Christ break relationship with his Father. When Jesus responds, "One does not live on bread alone," he not only puts physical and spiritual hunger in their proper order but also proclaims his total confidence in the Father to provide for his most essential hunger. Jesus, teach us to entrust the satisfaction of all our hungers to the Father.

Scripture: Deuteronomy 26:4–10; Psalm 91:1–2, 10–11, 12–13, 14–15; Romans 10:8–13; Luke 4:1–13

SECOND SUNDAY OF LENT

Becoming fully awake, they saw his glory. (Luke 9:32)

He Will Transform Our Lowly Bodies

In this Sunday's second reading, St. Paul proclaims that Christ "will change our lowly body to conform with his glorified body." In the gospel, Luke reports the mystery of Christ's Transfiguration. We read that up on the mountain, "Peter and his companions had been overcome by sleep, but becoming fully awake, they saw his glory." Today, many of Christ's followers are asleep when it comes to Christian teaching on the glorification of our bodies. We tend to have a superspiritual view of the afterlife as the state of the soul having been liberated from the body. But this is a Platonic view of things, not a Christian one. As St. John Paul II explains, the truth about man's destiny "cannot be understood as a state of the soul alone, separated (according to Plato: liberated) from the body but must be understood as *the definitively and perfectly 'integrated' state of man* brought about by a [perfect] union of the soul with the body" (TOB 66:5). St. Teresa of Avila wrote of being "utterly entranced" by a vision of Christ's glorified face and hands: "You will think . . . that it required no great courage to look upon hands and face so beautiful. But so beautiful are glorified bodies, that . . . those who see [them are rendered] beside themselves." Indeed, she insists that "if there were nothing in heaven to delight our sight other than the exalted beauty of glorified bodies, that would be enough." Lord, wake us up, that we may see your glory and be filled with hope in the glorification of our own bodies.

Scripture: Genesis 15:5–12, 17–18; Psalm 27:1, 7–8, 8–9, 13–14; Philippians 3:17–4:1; Luke 9:28b–36

THIRD SUNDAY
OF LENT

An angel of the LORD appeared to Moses in fire flaming out of a bush. As he looked on, he was surprised to see that the bush, though on fire, was not consumed.
(Exodus 3:2)

The Burning Bush and the Promised Land: Symbols of Mary

Since the time of St. Gregory of Nyssa, the theological tradition of the Eastern Churches has seen the burning bush described in the first reading as a symbol of Mary pregnant with the flame of Christ: *The burning bush seen by Moses / The prophet in the wilderness / The fire inside it was aflame / But never consumed or injured it / The same with the Theotokos / Mary Carried the fire of Divinity Nine months in her holy body* (Coptic prayer). Mary can also be seen in the first reading within the mystery of the Promised Land—for she too is "flowing with milk and honey." She is the fruitful land, the open flower that bore forth Christ with all the sweetness of her holy nectar. She is the one "acclaimed by all alongside the dearly beloved King, whom she suckled at her holy breasts," as the fourteenth-century mystic Hugh of Balma expressed it. As we read in this week's gospel, we too are expected to be a fertile land that bears sweet fruit. Let us pray to the gardener that he will "cultivate the ground . . . and fertilize it" (Lk 13:8) so that we may bear fruit in our lives. Mary, teach us how to say yes to God's life-giving flame as you did.

Scripture: Exodus 3:1–8a, 13–15; Psalm 103:1–2, 3–4, 6–7, 8, 11; 1 Corinthians 10:1–6, 10–12; Luke 13:1–9

FOURTH SUNDAY OF LENT

I shall get up and go to my father. (Luke 15:18)

Duty, Desire, and Destiny

Today's gospel reading relays the famous parable of the prodigal son. Based on the situation of the scribes and Pharisees to whom Christ addressed the parable, it is meant to convict those who are convinced of their own righteousness. In reality, the scribes and Pharisees are in danger of not entering the kingdom. The older son may have never disobeyed his father's orders, but the true nature of his father's heart actually angered him and made him rebel. Christ is trying to show the world that entrance into heaven is not merely a matter of "following all the rules." It's a matter of learning how to redirect our desire for fulfillment toward the Father's house (the Father's heart). What is so striking about the younger son is his *hunger*. That is what compelled him to leave, and that is what compelled him to return. When our hunger for fulfillment is misdirected, it leads to a life of "dissipation." But when our hunger is squashed in favor of merely following orders, it leads to a life of dutiful legalism that can easily become self-righteousness. There may be a glorious feast right before us, but if we aren't in touch with our hunger, we may "refuse to enter" as did the older son. And this is why, as St. Augustine put it, "he who loses himself in his passion is less lost than he who loses his passion." Why? Because it is precisely that hunger or passion that, when we "come to our senses," leads us to the Father.

Scripture: Joshua 5:9a, 10–12; Psalm 34:2–3, 4–5, 6–7; 2 Corinthians 5:17–21; Luke 15:1–3, 11–32

FIFTH SUNDAY OF LENT

So he was left alone with the woman before him.
(John 8:9)

Alone with Jesus and Loved in Our Sinfulness

This Sunday's gospel presents the story of Jesus' love and compassion for the adulterous woman. Try to picture the scene: somehow this woman had been caught in the very act of committing adultery. She had taken her longing for love, for union, for affirmation, and for intimacy to the wrong place. Not only is she laden with shame but also she's fearful for her life as she's brought before Christ by a crowd anxious to kill her by the insanely cruel and torturous method of hurling rocks at her. Christ utters his famous line: "Let the one among you who is without sin be the first to throw a stone at her." According to his own words, Jesus could have thrown a stone. But he came not to condemn; he came to save (see John 3:17). The gospel then tells us that Jesus "was left alone with the woman." What was that encounter like? Can we not imagine that in this moment the woman found in the divine Bridegroom the love she had wrongly sought elsewhere? Do you think when Jesus said, "Go, and from now on do not sin any more," that she might have turned and grumbled, "Who is this man to tell me what I can and cannot do with my body?" Or do you think, having encountered the love she was truly looking for, she left transformed, renewed, and affirmed in the deepest part of her being as a woman? In what areas of our hearts do we, like this woman, need to be alone with Jesus?

Scripture: Isaiah 43:16–21; Psalm 126:1–2, 2–3, 4–5, 6; Philippians 3:8–14; John 8:1–11

PALM SUNDAY OF THE LORD'S PASSION

My God, my God, why have you abandoned me?
(Psalm 22:2)

The Prayer of Agony

In the Palm Sunday psalm response, we recite with Christ his bitter prayer of agony from the Cross: "My God, my God, why have you abandoned me?" Once while on a personal retreat, getting in touch with a deep well of unfulfilled desire in me, I unleashed a torrent of rage at God and then swiftly went to confession for doing so. When the priest—an elderly monsignor who's spent a life very close to the heart of Jesus—heard my uncensored tirade, the first word out of his mouth was "good." Expecting the next word to be "confession," I was flabbergasted to hear him say "Good *prayer*." He continued: "What you felt in your heart was a share in what Jesus felt in his heart on the Cross. You expressed it in your way, and Jesus expressed it in his, but it's the same cry of the heart. In fact, what you experienced was Jesus *in you* crying out to the Father: 'My God, my God, *why have you abandoned me?*' You're learning to pray the prayer of agony. And it's not a prayer of doubt. It's a prayer of faith. You wouldn't be screaming at God if you didn't believe in him. You wouldn't be screaming at God if you didn't think he could hear you and rescue you. Same with Christ on the Cross." Then he concluded, "You don't need to confess that you were honest with God. You need to confess that you haven't been honest." Jesus, teach us how to open up the cry of our hearts to the Father just as you did.

Scripture: Luke 19:28–40 (at the procession with palms); Isaiah 50:4–7; Psalm 22:8–9, 17–18, 19–20, 23–24; Philippians 2:6–11; Luke 22:14–23:56

THE RESURRECTION OF THE LORD

They put him to death by hanging him on a tree. This man God raised on the third day. (Acts 10:39–40)

Easter Proclaims the Ultimate Goodness of the Body!

Ever since the entrance of death with the original sin, we have been tempted to contradict God's declaration on the seventh day that our bodily creation is good—in fact, "very good" (see Genesis 1:31). With the entrance of sin, we are tempted to think that the body is only good for suffering and dying, since that is our inevitable fate. Christ's Resurrection, as Pope Benedict XVI taught, means that "the universal law of death is not the world's final power after all and that it does not have the last word." In Christ's bodily Resurrection, Benedict XVI added that "God brings the approval of the seventh day of creation, his saying that all is good, to completion. . . . Resurrection means that through the twisted paths of sin and more powerfully than sin God ultimately says: 'It *is* good.'" John Paul II spoke of the diligent effort needed to overcome the "deep-seated habits" of Manichaeism (the heresy that our bodies are bad) in our way of thinking and acting. The bodily Resurrection of Christ crushes the Manichaean demon utterly. "They put him to death by hanging him on a tree," proclaims Peter in this Easter Sunday's first reading from the Acts of the Apostles. But this same man, Peter adds, "God raised on the third day." Lord, teach us how to enter into the bodily glory of Easter.

Scripture: Acts 10:34a, 37–43; Psalm 118:1–2, 16–17, 22–23; Colossians 3:1–4 (or 1 Corinthians 5:6b–8); John 20:1–9

SECOND SUNDAY OF EASTER/SUNDAY OF DIVINE MERCY

Jesus came and stood in their midst and said to them, "Peace be with you." (John 20:19)

Peace: the Fruit of Christ's Resurrection

Picture the scene: The disciples had locked themselves away and were afraid. The man they had been following for three years had just been hunted down, arrested, and executed. They were not only devastated but also fearful for their lives. Then, mysteriously, though the doors are locked, their "dead" Master appears in their midst. He is *alive* and standing before them in the flesh. Can you imagine all of the jaws dropping on the floor and the eyes watering in utter astonishment? Can you imagine the disciples waiting with baited breath for what he might have to say about all that has transpired? And then the first words out of his mouth are, "Peace be with you." What is this peace? Now can you imagine the disciples' confusion? Pope Francis offered this explanation of what the Lord said: "Christ has made all things one in himself: heaven and earth, God and man, time and eternity, flesh and spirit, person and society. The sign of this unity and reconciliation of all things in him is peace. Christ 'is our peace' (Eph 2:14)." God's eternal plan is the marriage of God and man, heaven and earth. But this marriage, this "oneness," could not happen until Christ descended into the darkest depths of our humanity (sin and death) and the darkest depths of the earth. When the risen Christ says "Peace be with you," he is saying all things have been reconciled and made one in him. The divine and human marriage has been consummated. The sign of this union is *peace*. Lord, grant us this peace.

Scripture: Acts 5:12–16; Psalm 118:2–4, 13–15, 22–24; Revelation 1:9–11a, 12–13, 17–19; John 20:19–31

THIRD SUNDAY OF EASTER

Simon, son of John, do you love me more than these?
(John 21:15)

What and Whom Do We Love?

In this Sunday's gospel, we hear the tender manner in which the risen Christ reinstates Peter after his three betrayals. Three times Jesus asks Peter, "Do you love me?" What does such a question mean? Peter had sinned grievously. We understand now that serious sin "destroys charity [love] in the heart of man . . . it turns man away from God, who is his ultimate end and his beatitude [bliss/happiness/fulfillment], by preferring an inferior good to him" (*CCC* 1855). This is a very illuminating definition of sin. The *Catechism* says we sin not when we prefer evil over good but when we prefer an inferior *good* to the supreme *Good*—God (the preference for the inferior good *is* the evil). In the moment of his betrayals, Peter preferred his own reputation and self-preservation (both good things) to the supreme Good. "Simon, son of John, do you love me?" Peter's yes indicates that Christ's Resurrection is already at work in his heart. He was allowing his love to be redirected toward the supreme Good. Peter, having experienced intimately the Lord's infinite love and mercy, is now able to share it with others: "Feed my lambs." Infinite Love is what every lamb is hungry for. Tragically, we often satisfy that hunger with lesser, finite loves. Peter witnesses to all of us that misdirected love can be redirected toward the Infinite Love we desire. Lord, redirect our love toward you!

Scripture: Acts 5:27–32, 40b–41; Psalm 30:2, 4, 5–6, 11–12, 13; Revelation 5:11–14; John 21:1–19

FOURTH SUNDAY OF EASTER

The Lamb who is in the center of the throne will shepherd them and lead them to springs of life-giving water. (Revelation 7:17)

The Eternal Bliss of Heaven

In this Sunday's second reading, we hear from the book of Revelation of St. John's vision of heaven. He sees a great multitude from "every nation, race, people, and tongue" standing before God's throne and worshipping him day and night. When I was growing up in Catholic schools, this sounded like eternal boredom. And for the privilege of this type of life in eternity, all I had to do was give up *everything* it seemed I really wanted! I would submit that the reason the secular world's promise of fulfillment looks so attractive is because it is plagiarizing the good things of God. When the world's pleasures are "sublimated" (rightly ordered and lifted up or made "sublime"), then they can be seen for what they are: so many foreshadowings of heavenly bliss. Then we can rejoice wholeheartedly with St. Brigid of Ireland in her description of heaven as "a great lake of beer" into which we'll dive with holy delight. Then we can get beyond squeamishness and take great joy in the prophet Isaiah's description of heaven as sucking deeply from the abundant breast of the "New Jerusalem" (an image of the Church as our Mother) and finding comfort in the overflow of her milk (see Isaiah 66:11–12). Then we can get beyond prudishness and joyfully recognize the erotic passion of the lovers in the Song of Songs as an image of the divine-human nuptials that await us in heaven (see Ephesians 5:31–32; Revelation 19–22). We worship whatever we think will satisfy our deepest hunger and thirst. What John saw was God satisfying that hunger and thirst day and night. Not eternal boredom. Eternal bliss! Lord, open our hearts to the real hope of this bliss.

Scripture: Acts 13:14, 43–52; Psalm 100:1–2, 3, 5; Revelation 7:9, 14b–17; John 10:27–30

FIFTH SUNDAY OF EASTER

I also saw the holy city, a new Jerusalem, coming down out of heaven from God, prepared as a bride adorned for her husband. (Revelation 21:2)

The Real Nuptials that Await Us in Heaven

This Sunday's readings speak of the consummation of the universe—"a new heaven and new earth"—as well as a new commandment to love one another as Christ has loved us. How does Christ love us? Freely, totally, faithfully, and fruitfully. Another name for this kind of love is *marriage*. Hence, from beginning to end, the Bible uses marriage more than any other image to help us understand divine love. Pope Francis said that it was "emblematic" that the book of Revelation describes the "final, definitive dimension" of our existence in terms of "the new Jerusalem, coming down out of heaven from God, prepared as a bride adorned for her husband" (Rv 21:2). It is the Church who is a bride with her Bridegroom. "And it is not just a manner of speaking: they will be real and true nuptials!" exclaimed Pope Francis.

"Yes, because Christ . . . has truly wed us and has made us, as a people, his bride. This is nothing more than the fulfillment of the plan of communion and love woven by God throughout history." Eternal Bridegroom, prepare us as a bride for your "mad eros"!

Scripture: Acts 14:21–27; Psalm 145:8–9, 10–11, 12–13; Revelation 21:1–5a; John 13:31–33a, 34–35

SIXTH SUNDAY OF EASTER

Whoever loves me will keep my word, and my Father will love him, and we will come to him and make our dwelling with him. (John 14:23)

The Body: God's Dwelling

In this Sunday's gospel we hear Jesus proclaim, "Whoever loves me will keep my word, and my Father will love him, and we will come to him and make our dwelling with him." The concept of God's "dwelling" has a rich and detailed history in biblical revelation. In the Old Testament the idea of God's dwelling passes through the mystery of the ark and the tabernacle to the Temple and the holy of holies. All of these mysteries culminate in Mary who, by conceiving the Son of God in her womb, became the dwelling place of God. Through Mary, a woman's body has become heaven on earth . . . God's dwelling place. This is the mystery of a woman's body. And this is why John Paul II teaches that *woman* is the model of the whole human race. She reveals what it means to be human: to be open to *receive* the fullness of God, to *conceive* the fullness of God, and to *bear* God into the world for others. This is the theology of a woman's body! What is the theology of a man's body? In all purity we can observe that man is called as "high priest" to enter the holy of holies and offer his flesh and blood there. Our bodies indeed proclaim a "great mystery"! Lord, open our eyes to it. Make your dwelling within us.

Scripture: Acts 15:1–2, 22–29; Psalm 67:2–3, 5, 6, 8; Revelation 21:10–14, 22–23; John 14:23–29

SEVENTH SUNDAY
OF EASTER

*That they may all be one, as you, Father, are in me and
I in you, that they also may be in us, that the world may
believe that you sent me. (John 17:21)*

Entering in to the Mystery of the Divine

This Sunday's gospel offers a kind of entrance into the
holy of holies: a little taste, for all those with tongues
to savor it, of the nectar of divine glory shared eternal-
ly between Father and Son. How does one acquire a
"tongue to savor it"? It's a mystical kind of sensitivity
that grows in us not so much from *thinking* but from
drinking. We must give ourselves permission to *feel*
the cry of the Bride in this weekend's second reading:
"Come!" And the Bridegroom responds, "Let the one
who thirsts come forward." Those who do will realize
the satisfaction of their deepest yearnings in Christ's
prayer to the Father "that they may all be one, as you,
Father, are in me and I in you, that they may also be
in us." Those with the courage to follow where that
powerful little word "in" leads will cross the threshold

of the divine intimacy, fulfilling Jesus' wish "that where I am they also may be with me, that they may see my glory that you gave me." Not only will we see the glory (the beauty, the joy, and the infinite radiation of love—goodness) that the Father has given the Son—but also the Son gives that same glory *to us*! "And I have given them the glory you gave me, so that they may be one, as we are one, I in them and you in me." Our bodies as male and female let us clearly know that we are called to be *one* with the Trinity: them in us and us in them. Jesus, take us "in" to this great mystery.

Scripture: Acts 7:55–60; Psalm 97:1–2, 6–7, 9; Revelation 22:12–14, 16–17, 20; John 17:20–26

PENTECOST SUNDAY

If the Spirit of the one who raised Jesus from the dead dwells in you, the one who raised Christ from the dead will give life to your mortal bodies also, through his Spirit that dwells in you. (Romans 8:11)

The Divine Spirit and the Human Body

This Sunday we celebrate the glorious feast of Pentecost. The *descent* of the Holy Spirit (the infinite life and love of the Trinity) on Mary and the apostles is the fruit of the *ascent* of Christ's humanity into the Trinity. O glorious exchange! O holy nuptials of divinity and humanity! We give God our humanity, and he gives us his divinity. We give God our finite body, and he gives us his infinite Spirit. But the body is not left behind to rot in favor of some purely spiritual eternity. Christ took his human body with him *into* God's eternity. And so, too, will we take ours. Pentecost is the celebration of the mortal body clothing itself in immortality, opening itself to the life of God, and receiving and conceiving that life within, in the pattern of Mary. As we read in one of the options for this Sunday's second reading, "If the Spirit of the one who raised Jesus from the dead dwells in you, the one who raised Christ from the dead will give life to your mortal bodies also." How? Precisely "through his Spirit that dwells in you." This is what it means to live "in the spirit" in the language of St. Paul. It does not mean we reject the flesh. It means we open our flesh to the life-giving Spirit. The flesh cut off from

God's Spirit leads to death. It *is* death. Pentecost is the promise that death is not the body's final word. If we open our bodies to the Holy Spirit's *descent*, our bodies will one day *ascend* into God's eternity. O Lord, show us the way to the eternal glorification of our bodies.

Scripture: Acts 2:1–11; Psalm 104:1, 24, 29–30, 31, 34; 1 Corinthians 12:3b–7, 12–13 (or Romans 8:8–17); John 20:19–23 (or John 14:15–16, 23b–26)

ORDINARY TIME

SOLEMNITY OF THE MOST HOLY TRINITY

*Hope does not disappoint, because the love of God
has been poured out into our hearts through
the Holy Spirit that has been given to us.
(Romans 5:5)*

Christian Hope Does Not Disappoint

The readings on Trinity Sunday invite us to hope for the fulfillment of our deepest, wildest, limitless desires. We all yearn for *something*, for some kind of lasting, infinite satisfaction. The Church calls this yearning *eros*. Fr. Peter John Cameron, a Dominican friar, points out that our yearning will either consume us or consummate us—depending on where we take it. The readings for today and the teaching of the Church remind us where we are headed: "God himself is an eternal exchange of love, Father, Son, and Holy Spirit, and he has destined us to share in that exchange" (CCC 221). That's it. That's all we really need to know. God is not a tyrant. He's not a slave driver. He's not trying to keep us from what we want. He's an infinite exchange of love and bliss. And he made us to participate in that glorious exchange. In fact, our bodies as male and female tell *this* story: the union of husband and wife foreshadows the glory that awaits us in the "wedding feast of the Lamb." This is what St. Paul is talking about when, in today's second reading, he boasts "in hope of the glory of God." And this "hope does not disappoint," St. Paul assures us. In other words, you're not crazy to have inexplicable, heart-rending hopes and desires. You are not wrong to believe there is something more. You will not be unhappy. Your fulfillment is coming. Your desire for *life* is not in vain. That is what we celebrate on Trinity Sunday. Father, Son, and Spirit, take us into your eternal exchange of love.

Scripture: Proverbs 8:22–31; Psalm 8:4–5, 6–7, 8–9; Romans 5:1–5; John 16:12–15

SOLEMNITY OF THE MOST HOLY BODY AND BLOOD OF CHRIST (CORPUS CHRISTI)

This is my body that is for you. . . . This cup is the new covenant in my blood. (1 Corinthians 11:24, 25)

The Feast that Satisfies Our Hunger for the Infinite

Today we celebrate the Solemnity of the Most Holy Body and Blood of Christ, or Corpus Christi Sunday. In the second reading, St. Paul recounts the words of the Lord: "This is my body that is for you. . . . This cup is the new covenant in my blood." Ponder this prayerfully: at the *source and summit* of everything we believe as Catholics is a mysterious *food* . . . a heavenly *bread*. This must mean that the very essence of our humanity is our hunger for Infinity. Fr. Harry Cronin, a Holy Cross priest, offers this reflection:

> Christ is a determined and deliberate lover. And this loving is done with bread.

He loves in bread and wine. For the dimmest fool will know that bread and wine are for hunger and thirst. And if hunger is fed with this bread, and thirst is slaked with this wine, then hunger and thirst for us will be holy. For hunger and thirst, basic and brutal, will gently jostle us toward the embrace of God. It is blunt and simple. It needs only careful, clear telling. Our God in Christ has become food because our God in Christ knows inside his own flesh every sad, tear-filled tale of hunger and thirst. He knows that the greatest hungering ache is the hungering for our beginning: for that crack of love's lightning that shot us into being. Which we find only in bread.

Lord, help us to find the satisfaction we yearn for in the bread you offer us. Amen.

Scripture: Genesis 14:18–20; Psalm 110:1, 2, 3, 4; 1 Corinthians 11:23–26; Luke 9:11b–17

TENTH SUNDAY IN ORDINARY TIME

Do not weep. (Luke 7:13)

Death Is Not the Final Word of the Body

In this Sunday's gospel, Jesus, moved with pity for a widow who lost her only son, says to her, "Do not weep." Then, interrupting the funeral procession, he proclaims, "Young man, I tell you, arise!" One of the main themes of St. John Paul II's Theology of the Body is that the human body has a language—it speaks, proclaiming the gospel mystery itself. And the gospel the body proclaims "is not of human origin," as St. Paul tells us in the second reading. It comes "through a revelation of Jesus Christ." What did Christ reveal in his body? He revealed the astoundingly glorious truth that, despite all indications to the contrary, death is not the final word proclaimed by the body. "See, your son is alive," announces Elijah in the first reading. Christ's Resurrection is the final word of the body. There is a time for mourning the death of those we love. Christ himself was "moved with pity" for the mother whose son had died. But let us never forget the final word of the body is not death. It is life . . . *eternal life!* "The dead man stood up and began to speak." Lord, give us hope in the resurrection of our bodies.

Scripture: 1 Kings 17:17–24; Psalm 30:2, 4, 5–6, 11, 12, 13; Galatians 1:11–19; Luke 7:11–17

ELEVENTH SUNDAY IN ORDINARY TIME

*Her many sins have been forgiven because
she has shown great love. (Luke 7:47)*

Religion of Law or Religion of Longing?

Today's gospel tells the story of the "sinful woman" who interrupts the gathering at the home of Simon the Pharisee and weeps at the Lord's feet. In response to Simon's indignation, Jesus asks him, "Do you see this woman?" Simon didn't *see* her. He couldn't *see* her. He was blinded by his own self-righteousness often associated with the Pharisees' rote "keeping of the law," which they thought gave them the right to look down on those who didn't. However, as we learn in the second reading, "a person is not justified by works of the law but through faith in Jesus Christ." Theologian Olivier Clément reflected on the vast difference between considering Christianity a religion of *law* versus what it truly is, a religion of *longing for the Infinite*. "In the Gospel the very root of sin," he observed, "is the pretense that we can save ourselves by our own effort." We have too often leaned heavily on our own supposed ability to "please God" by following the rules. Clément maintained that for "a moment we must lose our balance, must see in a flash of clarity . . . the ripping apart of our protective covering of happiness or moral virtue." If we allow ourselves to be stripped in this way, it will draw out of us "a cry of trust and love *de profundis*, from the depths of the heart." In other words, it will draw out of us faith in the One who loves us and who is the answer to our yearning for love. This is why the "sinful woman" came running to Jesus—she came to faith that he was the Infinite Love for which she had always longed." Your faith has saved you; go in peace," Jesus assures her. Lord, strip us of our protective covering so we can see ourselves as you see us.

Scripture: 2 Samuel 12:7–10, 13; Psalm 32:1–2, 5, 7, 11; Galatians 2:16, 19–21; Luke 7:36–8:3

TWELFTH SUNDAY IN ORDINARY TIME

There is neither Jew nor Greek, there is neither slave nor free person, there is not male and female; for you are all one in Christ Jesus. (Galatians 3:28)

In Christ There Is Not Male or Female

In today's second reading St. Paul proclaims, "There is neither Jew nor Greek, there is neither slave nor free person, there is not male and female; for you are all one in Christ Jesus" (Gal 3:28). The modern world promotes a vision of humanity that levels the sexual difference, erasing its essential meaning. Wouldn't these words from the letter to the Galatians seem to be a biblical justification? Rather, St. Paul concludes there is no longer male or female because they are "one in Christ Jesus." How do the *two* (male and female) become *one* in Christ Jesus? "For this reason a man shall leave his father and mother and cleave to his wife and the two shall become one flesh." St. Paul quotes this passage from Genesis 2:24 in his letter to the Ephesians and then adds, "This is a great mystery, and it refers to Christ and the Church" (Eph 5:32). The union of man and woman symbolizes union in Christ. But the only way the two can become one is through the sexual difference. Thus, St. Paul is not wiping away that difference. Rather, he's showing the fruit of that difference properly lived: unity in Christ. The great danger of being neutered is that we fail to see the divine mystery written in the sexual difference. And that's precisely why the devil is after our sexuality: to nullify the divine message it proclaims. Lord, give us eyes to see the mystery of your union with us, your Church, in the one-flesh union of husband and wife.

Scripture: Zechariah 12:10–11, 13:1; Psalm 63: 2, 3–4, 5–6, 8–9; Galatians 3:26–29; Luke 9:18–24

THIRTEENTH SUNDAY IN ORDINARY TIME

The flesh has desires against the Spirit, and the Spirit against the flesh; these are opposed to each other.
(Galatians 5:17)

Live by the Spirit and Not by the Flesh

In this Sunday's second reading, St. Paul contrasts living "by the Spirit" (good) with living "by the flesh" (not good). This does *not* mean, as many have sadly concluded, that St. Paul condemns the body or thinks of it as an inherent obstacle to living a "spiritual" life. As St. John Paul II proclaims so boldly in his Theology of the Body, the body is the specific vehicle of the spiritual life. In St. Paul's terminology "the flesh" refers to the whole person (body and soul) cut off from God's indwelling Spirit. It refers to a person dominated by vice. People who open themselves to life "in the Spirit" do *not* reject their body. Rather, they open their whole body-soul personality to divine inspiration. In this way, even our bodies "pass over" from death to life: "And if the Spirit of him who raised Jesus from the dead is living in you, he who raised Christ from the dead will also give life to your mortal bodies through his Spirit, who lives in you" (Rom 8:11). Lord, teach us how to open our flesh to your indwelling Spirit.

Scripture: 1 Kings 19:16b, 19–21; Psalm 16:1–2, 5, 7–8, 9–10, 11; Galatians 5:1, 13–18; Luke 9:51–62

FOURTEENTH SUNDAY IN ORDINARY TIME ·

Let all the earth cry out to God with joy. (Psalm 66:1)

Drinking Deeply from Heavenly Breasts

"Let all the earth cry out to God with joy," we proclaim in this Sunday's responsorial psalm. Joy in this life is the fruit of finding the true hope of satisfying the deepest desires of the heart. What is the first desire we all felt at birth if not hunger for the breast, hunger for mother's milk? In this Sunday's first reading, turning to the great feminine figure of Jerusalem, the prophet Isaiah uses this as an image of the fulfillment that awaits us in heaven: "Oh, that you may suck fully of the milk of her comfort, that you may nurse with delight at her abundant breasts!" The basic principle of St. John Paul II's Theology of the Body (which is also a basic principle of all of Christian theology) is that physical reality is a sign or icon of spiritual reality. When we let the icons of heavenly fulfillment lead us to the reality of heavenly fulfillment, the icons are doing their job. When we take our desire for heavenly fulfillment and aim this desire at the icon itself, the icon becomes an idol. Is this not the origin of the rampant idolatry of breasts in our world today? Our primordial hunger and thirst, our primordial yearning to be comforted, satisfied, delighted, and fulfilled, is revealed in the theology of the breast. This Sunday's gospel closes with words of great hope for those who know this hunger and thirst: "Rejoice because your names are written in heaven." Lord, teach us to rejoice in your promises and thus save us from all our idolatries.

Scripture: Isaiah 66:10–14c; Psalm 66:1–3, 4–5, 6–7, 16, 20; Galatians 6:14–18; Luke 10:1–12, 17–20

FIFTEENTH SUNDAY
IN ORDINARY TIME

Jesus Christ is the image of the invisible God.
(Colossians 1:15)

Your Body Makes Visible the Invisible

In this Sunday's second reading, St. Paul tells us that "Jesus Christ is the image of the invisible God." This brief statement itself proclaims the essential reality of the human body as a theology, a study of God. We cannot see God. He is invisible. And yet the *Catechism of the Catholic Church* tells us that "in the body of Jesus 'we see our God made visible and so are caught up in love of the God we cannot see'" (477). The human body's unimagined dignity is that it is the vehicle designed by God with the ability to communicate the divine mystery, to make visible the invisible. As St. John Paul II wrote, "The body, in fact, and only the body, is capable of making visible what is invisible: the spiritual and the divine" (TOB 19:4). This is how we are meant to see the human body—our own and every*body* else's. But we, the victims of a terrible degradation of the body, have been robbed, stripped of this vision, beaten, and left for dead like the man in the parable of this Sunday's gospel. Please, Lord, come and pour your healing oil and wine over our wounds just as the Good Samaritan did for the man beside the road. Enable us to see in your wounded and glorified body the image of the invisible God *and* the image of our own humanity— wounded but destined for glory. Amen.

Scripture: Deuteronomy 30:10–14; Psalm 69:14, 17, 30–31, 33–34, 36, 37 (or Psalm 19:8, 9, 10, 11); Colossians 1:15–20; Luke 10:25–37

SIXTEENTH SUNDAY IN ORDINARY TIME

God chose to make known the riches of the glory of this mystery among the Gentiles; it is Christ in you, the hope for glory. (Colossians 1:27)

The Hidden Mystery of God
Has Been Manifested

Today's second reading is jam-packed with nup-
tial-body theology! First, St. Paul says he is suffering
and filling up in his own flesh "what is lacking in the
afflictions of Christ on behalf of his Body, which is the
Church." Christ's sufferings aren't lacking, of course.
What is lacking is our willingness to bear them as
Christ's Body. We are his Body because we are his
Bride, his Church. It is the Bride who has become "one
body, one spirit" with Christ. Then St. Paul speaks of
"the mystery hidden from ages" that "has been manifest-
ed." What is this mystery? "It is Christ in you, the hope
for glory." Christ the Bridegroom is *in* us. Once again
we witness the power, the potency, and the intimacy of
that little word "in." Christ wants to be *in* us. Our bodies as male and female tell *this* story. As St. John Paul
II proclaimed, the body "has been created to transfer
into the visible reality of the world, the mystery hidden from eternity in God" (TOB 19:4). That mystery
hidden in God is Christ *in* the Father and the Father
in Christ and, in turn, through a sheer gift of grace,
us *in* Christ *in* the Father. This mystery of "in-ness" is

fulfilled superabundantly in Mary, the perfect model of the Church. Christ was literally *in* Mary (in her body, in her womb); Christ, after this model, is *in* his Church; and Christ is *in* us. Lord, help us to see this "great mystery" *in* our bodies.

Scripture: Genesis 18:1–10a; Psalm 15:2–3, 3–4, 5; Colossians 1:24–28; Luke 10:38–42

SEVENTEENTH SUNDAY IN ORDINARY TIME

And even when you were dead in transgressions and the uncircumcision of your flesh, he brought you to life along with him, having forgiven us all our transgressions.
(Colossians 2:13)

Bleeding Loins, Bleeding Heart, and the Fatherhood of God

In this Sunday's second reading, St. Paul speaks of the "power of God" that brings us to life even when we are "dead in transgressions and the uncircumcision of [our] flesh." Circumcision is a *central* biblical theme, yet it's rarely discussed. It just makes people uncomfortable. Sorry, we have to discuss it. Why was *this* the sign of the old covenant? It would seem God wanted to teach the men of Israel something the women already knew: participating in his fatherhood calls us to sacrifice our flesh and blood for others. Women bleed every month. They offer their bodies quite literally to their offspring. As we know from the new covenant, God is ultimately after the circumcision of our hearts—hearts ready to bleed for others. But it could not be more significant that the bleeding heart of the new covenant is foreshadowed by the bleeding loins of the old. Christ experiences both in order to reveal in his Body and Blood the true character of the Father. From the beginning, tempted by Satan's lie, we had come to conceive of God as a tyrant, as someone who wanted to *sacrifice us for himself*. The truth that Christ reveals in both his bleeding loins and his bleeding heart is that God wants to *sacrifice himself for us*. When Jesus teaches us the "Our Father" in today's gospel, he definitively rebukes Satan's lie and invites us to do the same. God is life-giving Love. He is *our Father*. Jesus, teach us how to see the mystery of the Father through your circumcised and crucified flesh.

Scripture: Genesis 18:20–32; Psalm 138:1–2, 2–3, 6–7, 7–8; Colossians 2:12–14; Luke 11:1–13

EIGHTEENTH SUNDAY IN ORDINARY TIME

Take care to guard against all greed, for though one may be rich, one's life does not consist of possessions.
(Luke 12:15)

Seek What Is Above: Long, Ache, and Pine for the Treasure of Heaven

In today's second reading, St. Paul urges us to "seek what is above . . . not what is on earth." Here St. Paul echoes the teaching of Christ recorded in Luke's gospel when he warns people not to "store up treasure for themselves" but to become "rich in what matters to God." I often think of that scene from *It's a Wonderful Life* when Clarence the angel says to George Bailey,

"Oh, we don't need money in heaven." And George responds, "Well it comes in pretty handy down here, bub!" Of course, the gospel does not condemn money or wealth in themselves. Rather, it warns against greed. "Take care to guard against all greed," says Jesus, "for though one may be rich, one's life does not consist in possessions." And St. Paul speaks of greed as idolatry. We all worship something. We worship whatever we think will satisfy our deepest desires. If we think money or possessions are what we're really looking for in life, we have yet to get in touch with the deepest part of ourselves: our "ache" and our "longing" for the Infinite. It is called *eros*, and it's a yearning for the ecstasy and bliss of what scripture calls the "wedding feast (or marriage) of the Lamb" (Rv 19:9). No one is as free as those who desire what they *really* desire. "You have made us for yourself, O God," says St. Augustine, "and our hearts are restless until we rest in you."

Scripture: Ecclesiastes 1:2, 2:21–23; Psalm 90:3–4, 5–6, 12–13, 14, 17; Colossians 3:1–5, 9–11; Luke 12:13–21

NINETEENTH SUNDAY IN ORDINARY TIME

Gird your loins and light your lamps. (Luke 12:35)

Be Ready to Open Immediately When the Bridegroom Comes

"Gird your loins and light your lamps," says Jesus in today's gospel, "and be like servants who await their master's return from a wedding, ready to open immediately when he comes and knocks." I suppose you know what your loins are. The lit lamp Jesus refers to means a heart ablaze with the fire Christ came to cast on the earth. Here, as surprising as it may seem to some, Christ is drawing a direct connection between our loins and our hearts. That connection is actually a central biblical theme: think circumcision of the flesh and circumcision of the heart (for the masculine image) and labor pains of the flesh and spiritual labor pains (for the feminine image). *Our bodies as male and female reveal spiritual mysteries.* This statement demands careful, prayerful attention. "The body and only the body," said St. John Paul II, "is capable of making visible what is invisible, the spiritual and the divine" (TOB 19:4). What spiritual message do our bodies proclaim? Christ, the eternal Bridegroom, wants to marry us. And he's coming. He's coming soon. Will we be ready, like a bride in waiting, to open to him when he comes? Lord, direct our hearts to yearn for your coming. Set us ablaze with your love. Amen.

Scripture: Wisdom 18:6–9; Psalm 33:1, 12, 18–19, 20–22; Hebrews 11:1–2, 8–19; Luke 12:32–48

TWENTIETH SUNDAY IN ORDINARY TIME

I have come to set the earth on fire, and how I wish it were already blazing! (Luke 12:49)

The "Mad Eros" of the Cross

"I have come to set the earth on fire," says Jesus in today's gospel, "and how I wish it were already blazing!" He then laments, "How great is my anguish until it is accomplished!" The second reading reveals his anguish:

"He endured the Cross, despising its shame." We find the key for interpreting this fire and this anguish in the great erotic love poetry of the scriptures, the Song of Songs: "Love is strong as death . . . a vehement flame" (8:6). "On the Cross, God's eros for us is made manifest," proclaims Pope Benedict XVI. "Eros is indeed . . . that force which 'does not allow the lover to remain in himself but moves him to become one with the beloved.' Is there more 'mad eros' . . . than that which led the Son of God to make himself one with us even to the point of suffering as his own the consequences of our offenses?" This "mad eros" took Jesus through a suffering one can't even begin to fathom. How great was his anguish indeed! But it was not suffering for its own sake. "For the sake of the joy that lay before him he endured the Cross." It's the joy of being one with his beloved, his Bride, the Church, and returning with her to the bosom of the Father. Lord, help us not to fear the fire of your "mad eros" that you came to cast upon the earth.

Scripture: Jeremiah 38:4–6, 8–10; Psalm 40:2, 3, 4, 18; Hebrews 12:1–4; Luke 12:49–53

TWENTY-FIRST SUNDAY IN ORDINARY TIME

I come to gather nations of every language; they shall come and see my glory. I will set a sign among them.
(Isaiah 66:18–19)

We Shall See His Glory

In this Sunday's first reading, we hear the following proclamation from the Lord through the prophet Isaiah: "I come to gather nations of every language; they shall come and see my glory. I will set a sign among them." John Paul II spoke of God's glory as the irradiation of his inner mystery. God wants to share himself with us. He wants to radiate his goodness to us. He wants to share his glory. He wants us to see and participate in his inner mystery. How is all of this possible? St. John Paul II tells us in the thesis statement of his Theology of the Body, "The body, in fact, and only the body, is capable of making visible what is invisible: the spiritual and the divine. It has been created to transfer into the visible reality of the world, the mystery hidden from eternity in God, and thus to be a sign of it"

(TOB 19:4). God gave the human body the capacity to reveal his own glory. Astounding. And it is all fulfilled through the Incarnation. All the more astounding! "The Word became flesh. . . . We have seen his glory" (Jn 1:14). Lord, teach us to see our bodies as a sign that reveals your glory.

Scripture: Isaiah 66:18–21; Psalm 117:1, 2; Hebrews 12:5–7, 11–13; Luke 13:22–30

TWENTY-SECOND SUNDAY IN ORDINARY TIME

You have approached Mount Zion and the city of the living God, the heavenly Jerusalem, and countless angels in festal gathering. (Hebrews 12:22)

We've Been Invited to an Eternal Wedding Banquet

In today's gospel, Jesus tells a parable about being invited to a wedding banquet. The parable seems a passing reference before Jesus gets to his point about humility later in the gospel. But whenever we read about weddings in sacred scripture, we should take note of their importance. From beginning to end, the Bible tells the story of marriage. Biblical scholar Dennis F. Kinlaw observed that when the Bible speaks of "the New Jerusalem coming down out of heaven 'prepared as a bride beautifully dressed for her husband' (Rv 21:2) . . . the human story that began with a wedding comes to its end; the wedding in the garden of Eden and every other wedding in human history . . . prefigured this end—a royal wedding—the one in which the Father gives a bride to his Son." This means that marriage, according to Kinlaw, was designed by God "to teach human creatures what human history is really all about." God wants to marry us. He's not an ogre or a tyrant or a cold legislator. He is an infinitely loving Bridegroom. This is what the second reading is getting at when it tells us not to fear some "gloomy darkness" in approaching God. "No, you have approached Mount Zion, the city of the living God, the heavenly Jerusalem"—these are all references to the Bride—"and Jesus, the mediator of a new covenant." The "new covenant" is a marriage proposal! God wants to be one with us forever in an intimacy beyond imagining. Mary, teach us how to say yes to this proposal as you did.

Scripture: Sirach 3:17–18, 20, 28–29; Psalm 68:4–5, 6–7, 10–11; Hebrews 12:18–19, 22–24a; Luke 14:1, 7–14

TWENTY-THIRD SUNDAY IN ORDINARY TIME

Whoever does not carry his cross and come after me cannot be my disciple. (Luke 14:27)

Christ Did Not Come to Save "Souls"

In today's first reading we hear that "the corruptible body burdens the soul" and in the responsorial psalm we read, "You turn man back to dust." The former attests to the burden of a life that yearns for the eternal but must accept the limitations and sufferings of earthly, bodily existence. The latter attests to the horror of death. It is *very* tempting in this situation to seek an un-Christian, even anti-Christian, "solution" to the conundrum of the tension that exists in us between body and soul. That very popular un/anti-Christian solution is to *dis-incarnate* the human being . . . to imagine that the real "us"—our real humanity—is the soul that lives on after death. By default, the body is then relegated to the realm of the subhuman. This is both *un-* and *anti*-Christian because Christ came in the flesh not to "save souls" (if by that we mean spirits snatched from their corruptible bodies) but to save *human persons* who are always, by divine design, a marriage of body and soul. "The proper Christian thing," as Pope Benedict XVI wrote before his election as pontiff, "is to speak not of the soul's immortality, but of the resurrection of the complete human being [body and soul] and of that alone." This is a very pricey redemption involving a bloody, bodily death, but it leads to a glorious bodily resurrection. As we learn in today's gospel reading, whoever does not "carry his own cross" and put Christ above everyone and everything else will not enter the glory he desires. Lord, help us to carry our cross in union with you so we might reach the glorious destiny your Cross opened up for us.

Scripture: Wisdom 9:13–18b; Psalm 90:3–4, 5–6, 12–13, 14–17; Philemon 9–10, 12–17; Luke 14:25–33

TWENTY-FOURTH SUNDAY IN ORDINARY TIME

"Take the fattened calf and slaughter it. Then let us celebrate with a feast, because this son of mine was dead, and has come to life again; he was lost, and has been found." Then the celebration began. (Luke 15:23–24)

The Prodigal Son and the Prodigal Father

Today's gospel presents the famous parable of the prodigal son. "Prodigal" describes someone who wastefully spends money or resources. But if you look up the term, you'll discover a second meaning: "prodigal" also refers to someone who *gives* something on a lavish scale. In light of this meaning, we could just as well call this the parable of the "prodigal father." We first see the father's prodigality in the fact that, when his son asks for his share of the inheritance (a request that implied he wished his father dead), the father actually gives it to him and, in this way, seems to finance his son's folly. What kind of father does such a thing? In our struggle with sin, we are often led to the question, *If you didn't want us to sin, why, God, did you make it possible for us to do so?* Cardinal Angelo Scola reflected, "Why did God the Father create man so radically free? Because he was not afraid—if it is permitted to speak in such terms—of the eventuality of sin, of human freedom going astray. Because the Father creates us in Jesus Christ, the incarnate Son who died and is risen." This means, Scola continued, that right from the beginning "the eventuality of sin is already included in his gratuitous and merciful design. God creates us in mercy; created freedom is redeemed freedom in the sense that, in the eventuality of sin, forgiveness is already offered to it 'in advance,' as the ever renewed possibility of returning to the Father's house." Scola was quick to point out that none of this means that sin loses "the terrible character of an offense against God and a mortal wound." But the emphasis is not placed on humanity's sin. It's placed on the Father's lavish (prodigal) plan of redemption. Father, may your prodigal love jostle our freedom to embrace the forgiveness you offer us for squandering the inheritance you've given us. Amen.

Scripture: Exodus 32:7–11, 13–14; Psalm 51:3–4, 12–13, 17, 19; 1 Timothy 1:12–17; Luke 15:1–32

TWENTY-FIFTH SUNDAY IN ORDINARY TIME

This is good and pleasing to God our savior, who wills everyone to be saved and to come to knowledge of the truth. (1 Timothy 2:3–4)

What Does It Mean to Be "Saved"?

In today's second reading, St. Paul writes to Timothy that God "wills everyone to be saved and to come to knowledge of the truth." This is good news indeed. But what does it mean? Saved from what? The truth about what? The stock answer is that we need to be saved from sin. True enough. But what does that mean? We tend to think about sin in juridical terms, as if sin were merely the transgression of a divine law. But that saps sin and our entire relationship with God of its true depth and meaning. When we put our "spousal lenses" on recalling that the whole Bible can be summed up with five words—*God wants to marry us*—the meaning of "sin," "salvation," and "truth" all *pop* and open us to the very depths of the meaning and purpose of human existence. The human being is *made for union with God* . . . deep, intimate union . . . "nuptial union" as the great mystic-saints tell us. But led astray by the Deceiver, we came to conceive of God not as the one who desires to fill us with the life and love for which we long but as one who is withholding something from us. Sin always involves the human attempt to satisfy our desire for God without God, apart from God. To be "saved from sin" we must come to "a knowledge of the truth" that God, far from holding out on us, wants us to be "filled with all the fullness of God" (Eph 3:19). Lord, save us from sin!

Scripture: Amos 8:4–7; Psalm 113:1–2, 4–6, 7–8; 1 Timothy 2:1–8; Luke 16:1–13

TWENTY-SIXTH SUNDAY IN ORDINARY TIME

Who dwells in unapproachable light, and whom no human being has seen or can see. (1 Timothy 6:16)

How to See the Invisible

In this weekend's second reading, St. Paul talks about the God who "dwells in unapproachable light," the God "whom no human being has seen or can see." Yet at the same time, he speaks about the "appearance of our Lord Jesus Christ." Holding these two seemingly irreconcilable truths together—God is invisible, but he has appeared in Jesus Christ—takes us right into the heart and center of what John Paul II meant by describing the human body as a "theology," a study of God. The *Catechism* tells us that God "impressed his own form on the flesh ... in such a way that even what was visible might bear the divine form" (CCC 704). Yes, God's mystery has been revealed in human flesh. For in Christ, "the whole fullness of deity dwells bodily" (Col 2:9). "Theology of the Body," therefore, is not only the title of a series of talks by John Paul II on sex and marriage. This phrase represents the very "logic" of the Christian faith. Your body and my body "has been created to transfer into the visible reality of the world, the mystery hidden from eternity in God, and thus to be a sign of it" (TOB 19:4). Is this the way you understand your body? If not, why not? Lord, open our eyes!

Scripture: Amos 6:1a, 4–7; Psalm 146:7, 8–9, 9–10; 1 Timothy 6:11–16; Luke 16:19–31

TWENTY-SEVENTH SUNDAY IN ORDINARY TIME

How long, O LORD? I cry for help but you do not listen! (Habakkuk 1:2)

The Vision Still Has Its Time; Wait for It!

In today's first reading, the prophet Habakkuk complains boldly and loudly that the Lord is not listening to his cry. He sees violence, destruction, ruin, misery, strife, and discord all around him, but the Lord seems to do nothing. Who can't relate? Look around our world today. Do we not see the same? And we needn't look far. Our own lives are often full of strife, ruin, discord, and violence. Look at the sexual and relational ruin and chaos all around us and within our own families! Do we, like Habakkuk, cry out to the Lord, "How long, O Lord? How long?" We should. And even if it seems as if the Lord is asleep on the boat, he will, at the right time, in the right way—a way that far exceeds anything we could hope for or imagine—answer our cry. "For the vision still has its time, presses on to fulfillment." What vision? The vision of God revealed through the human body. This is how God fully reveals himself—through the mystery of masculinity and femininity, through the very mystery under such violent attack today. At the beginning of the gospel, we have the Son of God, a male child, born of a woman. And at the end, a great sign will appear in the sky, a woman clothed with the sun and pregnant with eternal life for all who are open to the gift. This is the vision that "will not disappoint; if it delays, wait for it, it will surely come." Lord, we do believe. Help our unbelief.

Scripture: Habakkuk 1:2–3; 2:2–4; Psalm 95:1–2, 6–7, 8–9; 2 Timothy 1:6–8, 13–14; Luke 17:5–10

TWENTY-EIGHTH SUNDAY IN ORDINARY TIME

*I bear with everything for the sake of those who
are chosen, so that they too may obtain the
salvation that is in Christ Jesus.
(2 Timothy 2:10)*

To Be Chosen

In this Sunday's second reading, St. Paul writes from
his prison cell that he is bearing suffering "like a crim-
inal . . . for the sake of those who are chosen." Think
of how we *yearn* to be chosen, to be desired, and to be
recognized by others. And if the one who chooses us
is of great esteem, we feel all the more appreciated and
valued. Take a peasant girl who is chosen by a noble
king to be his beloved. She would feel deeply valued,
elevated, and elated. St. Paul is talking about being
"chosen" by the King of the universe. For what? John
Paul II tells us in his Theology of the Body that our
eternal election in Christ is fully revealed in the "great
mystery" of Ephesians 5:31–32, where St. Paul links
the union of spouses in "one flesh" with the union of

Christ and the Church. When we allow the grace of redemption to "untwist" what is disordered in our sexuality, we realize that our bodies tell the divine story of our being "chosen in Christ." Christ wants to marry us. He wants to be one with us and to share his glory with us forever. Our bodies tell this eternal love story! If we say yes to this eternal election, this eternal marriage proposal, we will "obtain the salvation that is in Christ Jesus together with eternal glory"—the glory of the royal wedding celebration. Let's say *yes*!

Scripture: 2 Kings 5:14–17; Psalm 98:1, 2–3, 3–4; 2 Timothy 2:8–13; Luke 17:11–19

TWENTY-NINTH SUNDAY IN ORDINARY TIME

Pray always without becoming weary. (Luke 18:1)

To Pray Always Is to Desire Always

Luke tells us that the purpose of the parable we hear in today's gospel reading is to teach us "the necessity

. . . to pray always without becoming weary." Is this even possible? It depends how we understand prayer. Pope Benedict XVI wrote, "The Fathers of the Church say that prayer, properly understood, is nothing other than becoming a longing for God." Let that sink in. The Christian life is never a matter of crushing our longings. It's a matter of redirecting them toward their true object. This is what prayer is. To "pray always," then, as today's gospel admonishes us to do, we must learn how to live within the painful "ache" of constant longing for heaven, for the "marriage of the Lamb." To the degree that we remain "attached" to the pleasures of this world, we have not yet learned to pray. "So brethren, let us long, because we are to be filled," wrote St. Augustine. "That is our life, to be trained by longing; and our training through the holy longing advances in the measure that our longings are detached from the love of this world." How do we pray *always*? St. Augustine concludes, "Desire is your prayer; and if your desire is without ceasing, your prayer will also be without ceasing. The continuance of your longing is the continuance of your prayer." Lord, teach us to pray.

Scripture: Exodus 17:8–13; Psalm 121:1–2, 3–4, 5–6, 7–8; 2 Timothy 3:14–4:2; Luke 18:1–8

THIRTIETH SUNDAY IN ORDINARY TIME

The Lord hears the cry of the poor. (Psalm 34:7)

The Womb of Mercy

"The Lord hears the cry of the poor," we proclaim in today's responsorial psalm. And this is also why the prayer of the Pharisee from the gospel is not received by God. We have no reason to believe he was lying about all his "righteous deeds" when he delighted that he was not like the tax collector. His collection of "righteous deeds," however, became a source of pride that blinded him to his poverty before God. And if you, like me, have found yourself being harsh with the Pharisee in this parable ("Well, thank God I'm not like that Pharisee who looks down on others"), aren't you, like me, guilty of looking down on him? Mercy. We are *all* in need of it. And that's precisely the point: we're all in the same boat, and in case you haven't noticed, the boat is sinking. The Hebrew word for mercy (*rahamim*) is closely related to the word "womb." A woman's body reveals mercy as an experience of being reborn into the divine milieu of unconditional love. What's my milieu? Is it unconditional love and forgiveness? Or is it love *if* . . . forgiveness *if . . . ?* If what? If I'm worthy of it? If I perform well? If I'm not really "*that* bad"? Whenever I catch myself trying to justify myself by my own merits, I can be sure that somewhere in my heart I don't really believe in God's unconditional love. If I did, I wouldn't be striving so hard to earn it. Babies in the womb don't need to earn love. And from within the womb of mercy, nor do we. Lord, show us your merciful love.

Scripture: Sirach 35:12–14, 16–18; Psalm 34:2–3, 17–18, 19, 23; 2 Timothy 4:6–8, 16–18; Luke 18:9–14

THIRTY-FIRST SUNDAY
IN ORDINARY TIME

For you love all things that are and loathe
nothing that you have made; for what you

hated, you would not have fashioned.
(Wisdom 11:24)

God Is Fathering Us Right Now

Living the theology of our bodies means learning to live in right relationship with God, ourselves (our *bodily* selves), every*body* else, and the rest of creation. Today's first reading from the book of Wisdom has much to teach us in this regard. "For you love all things that are and loathe nothing that you have made, for what you hated, you would not have fashioned. And how could a thing remain unless you willed it?" None of us asked to exist. Our existence is the pure prerogative of the Creator. However, we were not only created in the womb. The "lover of souls" is fathering us right this very moment, holding us in existence by an act of his loving will ("how could a thing remain, unless you willed it?"). And we can and should assent to that. We can and should learn to align our wills with God's creative will for our existence, and for all of creation. In this way, we come to recognize, as the first reading invites us to do, that God's "imperishable spirit is in all things." Encountering God "does not mean fleeing this world or turning our back on nature," as Pope Francis reminds us. For through the Incarnation, God has "entered into the created cosmos, throwing in his lot with it." And this means that from "the beginning of the world . . . the mystery of Christ is at work in a hidden manner in the natural world as a whole." Jesus, help us to see how you are at work in the mystery of the natural world.

Scripture: Wisdom 11:22–12:2; Psalm 145:1–2, 8–9, 10–11, 13, 14; 2 Thessalonians 1:11–2:2; Luke 19:1–10

THIRTY-SECOND SUNDAY IN ORDINARY TIME

The children of this age marry and remarry;
but those who are deemed worthy to attain
to the coming age and to the resurrection
of the dead neither marry nor are given
in marriage. (Luke 20:34–35)

We Are Made for the Nuptials of Eternity

Today's gospel reading contains one of the three key words of Christ from which John Paul II developed his Theology of the Body. Jesus asserts that in the Resurrection, we "neither marry nor are given in marriage." This only makes sense in light of the overall biblical story that God wants to marry us. The Bible begins with the marriage of man and woman, but it ends with the marriage of Christ and the Church. Earthly marriage—as beautiful and wonderful as it can be—can never satisfy that "ache" within us for the Infinite. Human love is not our be-all and end-all. We are made for the divine. What earthly marriage *can* be and is *meant* to be is a sacrament of the divine, an earthly preparation for the "marriage of the Lamb." But you no longer need sacraments *of* heaven when you're *in* heaven. People often ask, "Does this mean I won't be with my spouse in heaven?" Assuming both spouses say yes to God's wedding invitation, they will certainly be together. All who respond will live together in a communion that fulfills superabundantly all that is true, good, and beautiful about marriage and family life here on earth. In other words, marriage is not *deleted* in the Resurrection. It's taken up, fully redeemed, and *completed* in the nuptials of eternity. Then, as today's psalm response has it, our "joy will be full!" Lord, direct our desire according to your design so we are aimed at our destiny. Amen.

Scripture: 2 Maccabees 7:1–2, 9–14; Psalm 17:1, 5–6, 8, 15; 2 Thessalonians 2:16–3:5; Luke 20:27–38

THIRTY-THIRD SUNDAY IN ORDINARY TIME

By your perseverance you will secure your lives.
(Luke 21:19)

Wars, Famines, Earthquakes, Plagues, and Persecutions—and Then Comes the Bride

Today's readings warn of great calamities that will come upon the world before Christ's return: "The day is coming," says the prophet Malachi, "when the proud and all evildoers will be stubble." It's a day "blazing like an oven" that "will set them on fire." And Christ warns in the gospel of wars, famines, earthquakes, plagues, and persecutions. We can consider these the labor pains of a new birth for God's people. "The Church will enter the glory of the kingdom only through this final Passover, when she will follow her Lord in his death and Resurrection," teaches the *Catechism of the Catholic Church* (677). This is how victory happens. As scary as it is, we must all—in one way or another—follow Christ the whole way through his passion and death in order to come out the other side in the glory of his Resurrection. In this way, the whole world will witness "God's victory over the final unleashing of evil, which will cause his Bride to come down from heaven . . . after the final cosmic upheaval of this passing world" (CCC 677). Then "there will arise the sun of justice with its healing rays," and we will consider all the labor pains as "nothing" compared to the glory of God revealed through the beauty of the Bride. Jesus, grant us the grace of perseverance in our trials, that they may lead us to you. Amen.

Scripture: Malachi 3:19–20a; Psalm 98:5–6, 7–8, 9; 2 Thessalonians 3:7–12; Luke 21:5–19.

SOLEMNITY OF OUR LORD JESUS CHRIST, KING OF THE UNIVERSE

He is the image of the invisible God. (Colossians 1:15)

This King Is the Image of the Invisible God

Today we celebrate the Solemnity of Christ the King. Who is this king? In the second reading, St. Paul proclaims, "He is the image of the invisible God." Pause. That is *astounding*. God is invisible. Pure spirit. How can the invisible God be imaged? How can the invisible God be made visible? It is called Christmas. Incarnation. St. John tells us in his first letter that he has *seen* what he proclaims to us, he's *touched* it with his hands, the eternal Word of the Father (see 1 John 1:1). How? "The Word became flesh ... we saw his glory" (Jn 1:14). This makes the human body not only something biological but also something theological—it reveals the very logic, the *logos* of God. And on the Cross, his dying body reveals the logic of God's kingship, a logic totally "other" than that to which we are accustomed. Worldly kings use their power to stay on top. But this king freely places himself among the lowest of the low. "If you are King of the Jews, save yourself," jeer the soldiers in the gospel. But only by embracing death could he be "the firstborn from the dead," as St. Paul proclaims him. This king brings "peace by the blood of his cross." Jesus, you grant us peace, not as the world grants it but through another kind of kingship. Show us in and through your crucified and risen flesh the meaning of peace, and bring us into your kingdom. Amen.

Scripture: 2 Samuel 5:1–3; Psalm 122:1–2, 3–4, 4–5; Colossians 1:12–20; Luke 23:35–43

SUGGESTIONS FOR FURTHER STUDY

+ If you have the aptitude, read St. John Paul II's actual text: *Man and Woman He Created: A Theology of the Body* (Pauline, 2006). If you need help with that, read it in conjunction with my extended commentary *Theology of the Body Explained* or my *Theology of the Body for Beginners*. Visit my ministry's website corproject.com and click on "shop" for a full listing of additional resources.

+ Explore what other authors and teachers have written about the Theology of the Body. There are so many good resources out there today, each with their own emphases and insights. Do an internet search of "theology of the body resources" to find them.

+ If you would like ongoing formation in the Theology of the Body, consider joining a worldwide community of men and women who are learning, living, and sharing the TOB as members of the Cor Project. Visit cormembership.com to learn more.

+ Consider taking a five-day immersion course through the Theology of the Body Institute. Learn more at tobinstitute.org.

+ For more in-depth study, consider the Theology of the Body Institute's certification program or the graduate degree programs offered by the Pontifical John Paul II Institute for Studies on Marriage and Family.

Christopher West serves as senior lecturer of theology and Christian anthropology for the Theology of the Body Institute. His global lecturing, bestselling books, and multiple audio and video programs have made him one of the world's most recognized teachers of John Paul II's Theology of the Body. As founder and president of The Cor Project, he leads an international outreach devoted to helping others learn, live, and share this teaching.

West is the author of more than a dozen books, including *Theology of the Body Explained*, *Theology of the Body for Beginners*, and *Good News about Sex & Marriage*. His work has been featured in the *New York Times*, on ABC News, MSNBC, and Fox News, and in countless Catholic and evangelical media.